The Good Man's Survival Guide

How To Recognize and Avoid A No Good Skeezer

EMAIL ANY COMMENTS TO:
JDUVALSERIES@YAHOO.COM

WEBSITE:
WWW.MYSPACE.COM/JDUVALSERIES

The Good Man's Survival Guide

How To Recognize and Avoid A No Good Skeezer

J. DUVAL

LOS ANGELES  CALIFORNIA

Copyright © 2005 by J. Duval
Los Angeles, California
All Rights Reserved
Printed and Bound in the United States of America

Published and Distributed by:
Milligan Books, Inc.

Cover Layout by Kevin Allen
Interior Design by Caldonia Joyce
Graphic Images by Afrocentrix

First Printing, August 2005
10 9 8 7 6 5 4 3 2 1

ISBN: 0-9767678-8-0

Milligan Books
1425 W. Manchester Blvd., Suite C
Los Angeles, CA 90047

www.milliganbooks.com
drrosie@aol.com
(323) 750-3592

All rights reserved. No part of this book may be reproduced in whole or in part, in any form or by any means, electronic or mechanical, including photocopying, recording or by any information storage and retrieval system, without permission in writing from the author.

A GOOD MAN'S PRAYER

Give me the EYES to SEE
everything around me;

a BRAIN to THINK
about the things that I SEE;

a MOUTH to SPEAK
the truth that I am THINKING;

and the WISDOM to DISCERN
the difference between

A **GOOD** Woman and A **NO GOOD** Skeezer

Amen

TABLE OF CONTENTS

Acknowledgments xi
Introduction xiii

CHAPTER ONE
SuckerMan 1

CHAPTER TWO
What Is a Skeezer? 4

CHAPTER THREE
What Does a Skeezer Want? 6
Skeezer and SuckerMan 6

CHAPTER FOUR
How to Identify and Flip the Script on a Skeezer .. 7

CHAPTER FIVE
How to Rid Yourself of a Skeezer 11

CHAPTER SIX
Good Men are Ample, Fools & Players Wanted ... 12

CHAPTER SEVEN
Am I a Good Woman or Just Another Skeezer? .. 15

CHAPTER EIGHT
Potential Mate Value (PMV) Chart 17

A GOOD MAN'S SURVIVAL GUIDE

CHAPTER NINE
    Pre-season - 20
        September 6th through October 30th
    Dear Hunting Season 20
        1st quarter - 21
        October 31st through November 30th
        2nd quarter - 21
        December 1st through December 24th
        Halftime Show - 21
        December 25TH
        3rd quarter - 22
        December 26th through January 15th
        4th quarter - 22
        January 16th through February 14th
        Off Season - 23
        February 15th through September 5th

CHAPTER TEN
    Emotionally Stuck on Stupid
    and No Good for You 24

CHAPTER ELEVEN
    Whoso Findeth a Wife Findeth a Good Thing 29

CHAPTER TWELVE
    The Baker's Dozen 32
        Ms Pigeon 35
        Ms Drama Queen 38
        Ms Begga Lott 41
        Ms Independent 44
        Ms Holy Roller 48
        Ms Holy Hustler 53
        Ms Package Deal 56

Table of Contents

    Ms Gold Digger 59
    Ms Playing Hard To Get 62
    Ms Party Girl 65
    Ms Will Not Call 68
    Ms N. Dee Nile 71
    Ms Waited Too Long 74

CHAPTER THIRTEEN
    How to Translate for a Good Man 78

CHAPTER FOURTEEN
    If you Have to Pay, It's All About Her 82

CHAPTER FIFTEEN
    Does She Genuinely Want to be Your Friend? ...86

CHAPTER SIXTEEN
    Dah Playaz Klub – We Get Ours and Then Some .89
        Charm Her 91
        Couch Potato 92
        No Mo' Money 93
        Sugar Daddy 94
        Pulpit Pimp 95
        Player 97
        Mama's Boy 98
        Gigga Her Lo 99
        Handy Man 100
        Procrastinator 101
        Won't Let Go 102
        Down Low 103

CHAPTER SEVENTEEN
    Busy or Unavailable is Just an Excuse 104

CHAPTER EIGHTEEN
   The Key to Peace of Mind, Productivity and
   Longevity is Cleansing 108

ACKNOWLEDGMENTS

My heart goes out to all of the good men who have suffered "mentally, physically and financially" and are still suffering today from the scandalous behavior of those "No Good Ass Skeezers." I know that some of those men will never recover financially in their lifetime. I thank God that I was never that severely bitten and experienced only disappointment rather than financial pain and suffering from Skeezers.

I want to thank the following people for taking out the time to review my notes, scribbles and graphics, as well as provide their input as I was putting it together: Verona Nelson, Carla Glover, Mr. Ambassador Perkins and numerous others whose names I haven't mentioned, but who are not forgotten.

I want to thank Rita Ellison of Just That EZ Financing in Los Angeles (on the Crenshaw strip) for her financial guidance and assistance and The Serving Spoon Restaurant in Inglewood, CA. for allowing me to take the time to sit, listen, observe and write about many of the personalities in this guide.

I want to thank all of the GOOD women out there whom I have met over the years, because if it were not for you, I would not have known the difference between a "Good Woman" and a "No Good Ass Skeezer."

Finally, I want to thank all of you Skeezers out there, that I came in contact with over the years because if it were not for you, this guide would not exist.

INTRODUCTION

This guide is based upon years of experience, observation and testimonials and is to be used to assist good men in identifying and eliminating Skeezers that not only use (or attempt to use) them, but who ruin the opportunity for good women to establish meaningful relationships with them.

Where are most of the good men today? They have allowed themselves to be held captive—physically, mentally & financially—by "abusive," "lazy," "inconsiderate," "irresponsible" and "lying" Skeezers that pretend to be good women.

How did those good men allow that to happen? They evolved over a period of generations into what has been called the gentleman. What is a gentleman? A gentleman is a good man that has been:

- ✓ trained to serve and obey the woman.
- ✓ trained to tell a woman what she wants to hear.

- ✓ trained to work himself to death simply to please the woman.
- ✓ trained to think like a slave by doing the most and expecting the least.
- ✓ trained to give a woman whatever she wants to keep her happy and/or shut her up.
- ✓ trained in soliciting for prostitution (i.e., give her what she wants in exchange for sex).
- ✓ trained that accepting physical, emotional and financial abuse from a woman is being a man.
- ✓ trained to de-value himself by having to prove his worthiness to a woman he meets, without requiring the same of her

This does not represent every good man. This only represents the majority of good men that have sacrificed the pursuit of "life, liberty, prosperity and peace-of-mind" for a "No Good Ass Skeezer."

The good men have been programmed and trained, from the cradle, to see the woman as a human slot machine. Put their money and deeds into her and **HOPE** that he eventually

Introduction

come out a winner, while she receives **IMMEDIATE** gratification through his money and deeds (i.e., wining, dining, entertaining, repairing, taking her on trips, buying her things, helping her out with her bills that she foolishly and selfishly created to receive immediate gratification at that time for herself). At no time is he told that he is supposed to receive **IMMEDIATE** gratification for what he wants from her, but rather **WAIT** until she is ready, which she is given the option to do or not do.

Unfortunately, the good women out there know who these Skeezers are, because a lot of them are their friends. By accepting and not condemning those Skeezers behavior, the good women allow Skeezers to destroy the possibility for them and other good women to establish a meaningful relationship with a good man.

To the good men that aren't held captive, trust me when I say that these guidelines will allow you to recognize and avoid a Skeezer and live a more Peaceful and Prosperous life. The key is avoiding them once you recognize them.

To the Players out there, you already know what to do and are doing it quite well. I am sure that many of you started out as good men until you were bitten by one or more Skeezers as well.

CHAPTER ONE

Could this possibly be you? Who is this SuckerMan? You, if you are that stupid. No matter how you think you look, this is how a Skeezer sees you.

SuckerMan is helpful, funny, sensitive, a friend, a good listener and a dumb ass fool. That is what a Skeezer thinks of SuckerMan. Take a good, long, close look and make sure this never becomes you.

- ✓ She doesn't care about him.
- ✓ She will tell him what to do.
- ✓ She will knowingly take advantage of his interest in her.

A GOOD MAN'S SURVIVAL GUIDE

- ✓ He is always available for her, but she isn't for him.
- ✓ He foolishly and freely spends his money on her.
- ✓ She tells him that she is not interested in a relationship (with him of course).
- ✓ He never gets the booty and she knows that he never will.
- ✓ He runs errands for her. He repairs things in her home and car at no charge.
- ✓ She tells him that she doesn't ever want to lose his friendship.
- ✓ She will contact him when she is bored and has nothing else to do.
- ✓ She constantly reminds him of what a nice and sweet man he is.
- ✓ He knows she isn't interested in him but he hopes she eventually changes her mind.
- ✓ She complains to him about other men and how bad they treat her.

If any (or all) of the above applies to you, then change your ways, dump those Skeezers immediately and don't ever allow yourself to think or behave like this again.

CHAPTER TWO

WHAT IS A SKEEZER?

This is what's on the inside. It's the outward appearance that will deceive most good men. She is capable of taking on various outward appearances, so you have to be able to recognize her by her attitude and behavior. Don't allow her to get a bite out of your life.

A Skeezer is an angry, emotionally unstable, and psychologically disturbed impersonator and predator that will typically blame men for the immature and irresponsible choices that she has made in her life.

A Skeezer assumes, with fraudulent intent the character of a good woman so she can prey on (not pray) and use good men to support her selfish, irresponsible and inappropriate lifes

What Is A Skeezer?

tyle. By the way, Skeezers will also use their children or get pregnant if they have to. There are no limits to what a Skeezer will do to get what she wants.

CHAPTER THREE

WHAT DOES A SKEEZER WANT?

Don't be so foolish or stupid!! This is what a Skeezer wants and not you.

Skeezer and SuckerMan
(Their Thoughts)

CHAPTER FOUR **4**

How to Identify and Flip the Script on a Skeezer

(They usually never say no to a free meal)

Here's a tip on identifying a female who is a Skeezer (one that has no respect for you AND is just "killing time" and/or "looking for an opportunity to get you to spend your money on her"). This would have to be done at a restaurant where the individual brings the menu to you and you pay after the meal is finished. Remember, you won't know this until you get her to a restaurant and ask her the right question.

1. Agree to meet at a restaurant. Do not pick her up and do not mention paying for the date.

A GOOD MAN'S SURVIVAL GUIDE

2. When you get the menu and are ready to order, "let her order for herself" (this is very important)

3. Let the conversation flow and at some point (just prior to the meal being paid for), look her directly in her eyes (do not look away) and ask her if she wants to see you again, and if so will she pick up the next tab? Do not say another word afterwards until she gives you an answer, and if she says "excuse me?" chances are she as no genuine interest in you. If she asks you to repeat what you said, say exactly the same thing again. Do not allow her to change the conversation to another subject. If she resists responding to your question or says she doesn't want to see you again, or if she says that she doesn't believe in paying so soon, simply pay only your portion and not hers. You are being used as a SuckerMan (i.e. a Fool) to "kill time" and "get A free meal." The restaurant cannot make you pay for her meal because you did not order for her

4. After you pay your portion simply be polite, offer to walk her to her car and if she says no, get away from her and consider yourself fortunate that you weren't another SuckerMan. See it as a victory because you had an opportunity to get out, you had a nice meal, you only paid for yourself and you've learned "how to identify and flip the script on a hungry Skeezer."

This tactic is to be only used on a female that has no interest in you and is only using you to kill time or get a free meal. Understand clearly that a fair, considerate and unselfish female would have no problem paying for the next date and if she was not interested in you (which she will know before the date is over), she should pay her own way since she now knows there will not be anymore dates.

Remember, if she isn't interested in you and will not tell you that, or will not pay for her portion of the date, then she has no respect for you, so any tactic you use on her to avoid wasting your money is justified.

Finally: There are a lot of experienced, scandalous Skeezers that are quick enough to sense that she needs to tell you what you want to hear, in order to get you to pay for the meal. If that's the case and you aren't experienced enough to detect that, then I suggest that you at least keep the cost of each of the first few dates under $ 30.00, just in case you do pay and don't see her again, or if she is not interested in you. You would not have to pay an admission fee to spend time with a good woman because she will be interested in and considerate of you.

CHAPTER FIVE

How to Rid Yourself of a Skeezer

Has she gotten on your last nerve? Do you feel stuck or trapped? Well, if you do, then give her some of your A.S.S. to relieve your stress.

Anti Skeezer Spray
Colorless & Odorless. She Won't Know You Applied It.

Also Repels and Irritates: Bitches, Leaches, Chicken Heads, Gold Diggers and Hood Rats.

WARNING: This causes Crack Heads to react in a violent manner. Do not try this on one of them; you may get your ASS WHIPPED.

FPA Tested
(Federal Players Association)

Ingredients:
Common Sense, Fairness, Reason & Unselfishness

Will Not Cause Harm To:
Children, Pets, Pussified or Pussy Whipped Men

CHAPTER SIX

GOOD MEN ARE AMPLE, FOOLS & PLAYERS WANTED

A good man is a wise man and a wise man is no fool. Your first impression will be a lasting impression. If you begin behaving like a fool, trying to impress a woman by spending money and buying gifts, you will have to continue to act like a fool. She will not be looking at your character, she is now looking at your money. So if you don't know what happens to a fool and his money, then act like one, and you will soon see.

Many good men have been trained to behave like dogs and submit to the following commands which are: "Sit", "Be Silent", "Fetch (the Money)", "Bring it to me (the Money)" while many no good women continue to take advantage of them. When a man speaks the truth about abusive treatment, selfish, lazy and no good women he is told "where are you meeting these women" and he is considered angry and bitter. When a woman speaks the truth about abusive treatment, selfish, lazy and no good men she is praised for speaking out and letting others know about these types of men. Why is that? The answer is because most good men aren't valued beyond their wallets or deeds and they allow themselves to be brainwashed to think that they are to over-extend themselves and even suffer for any woman's benefit.

Most women don't want a good man; they want a challenge, money, romance. They want:

1. A man that is unavailable and has one or more women so she can compete for him

2. A man that will support their irresponsible behavior and/or

3. A man that will fulfill their romantic fantasies of wining, dining and freely spending his money on them. What they don't seem to realize (or want to realize) is that certain personalities are usually associated with that behavior.

Here are 3 male personalities that I have noticed:
Controlling – He spends his money on her and he wants her available to him, when

needed. He spends the cash so he calls the shots. She is there for the ride so she should enjoy it while it lasts.

Insecure – He feels as if he has to spend money or buy her things to be with her. He will not be a decision maker in a relationship and especially when it comes to making major decisions.

Ladies Man – He is secure with himself and is just accustomed to spending money on women and enjoying their company. He has no problem with doing so and does it on a regular basis. He will never expect her to be the only woman once he gets her and he will always have at least one woman on the side.

These men are neither right nor wrong, they are simply who they are, so accept them and don't try to change them. You won't be able to separate the spending from the personality because "it's a packaged deal."

If women want a good man then I suggest that they start behaving like a good woman. What are some of the qualities of a good woman? Just continue to read and you will see.

CHAPTER SEVEN

AM I A GOOD WOMAN OR JUST ANOTHER SKEEZER?

Some women have no clue what a good woman is because most men either don't know or don't tell them. Here are some positive and basic qualities that any good woman can and should consistently display. Don't settle for less!!

Am I a Good Woman?

or just another Skeezer?

- ✓ She is not looking for you to take care of her.
- ✓ She is emotionally free and psychologically healthy.

A GOOD MAN'S SURVIVAL GUIDE

- ✓ She has healthy relationships with those close to her.
- ✓ She will not bring drama, stress or debt into your life.
- ✓ She is financially responsible and manages her money well.
- ✓ She can sensibly communicate her likes and dislikes to you.
- ✓ She was happy and content with herself before she met you.
- ✓ She is happy just being in your company doing and saying nothing.
- ✓ She does not have to run the streets and clubs in order to be happy.
- ✓ She does not expect for you to be perfect and does not try to change you.
- ✓ She can keep your business private and not become a public embarrassment.
- ✓ She is seeking companionship to enhance her happiness and not to make her happy.
- ✓ She knows how to cook and is not expecting to dine out most of the time.

CHAPTER EIGHT

Potential Mate Value (PMV) Chart

This applies only to females who considers themselves to be single, available and unattached.

CATAGORY	EXPLANATION	POINTS TAKEN AWAY
Age	As age increases, so does her willingness to become inflexible with a man. **Deduct 1 point for every 5 years above the age of 30.** (Ex.: 35 = 1, 40 = 2, etc.)	
Attitude	Selfish, unreasonable and inconsiderate when interacting with you. She does not value you and expects you to do most (if not all) of the planning, initiating contact with her and paying. **Deduct 1 point.**	
Domestic Skills	She has no domestic skills. She can't cook, is not organized and prefers to dine out most of the time. **Deduct 1 point.**	

A GOOD MAN'S SURVIVAL GUIDE

CATAGORY	EXPLANATION	POINTS TAKEN AWAY
CHILDREN	You will never come first as long as there is a child in the home. Eventually you will be expected to contribute time & expenses to the child. **Deduct 1 point for each child in the home.**	
EMOTIONAL LIABILITY	She is not emotionally free. She is still attached to someone or something in her past and refuses to let go. **Deduct 1 point.**	
FINANCIAL LIABILITY	Credit is bad, does not pay her bills on time, financially over-extended, and living beyond her means. **Deduct 1 point.**	
UNDESIRABLE LOCATION	Lives at a distance that makes it inconvenient for the two of you to see each other on a regular basis (i.e., during the weekdays as well as weekends). **Deduct 1 point.**	
PHYSICALLY UNAVAILABLE	Too busy (or pretends to be too busy) when it comes to spending time with you. It does not matter what the reason is—you can't get to know her if she is unavailable. **Deduct 1 point.**	
UNEMPLOYED	She does not have a steady job or any steady source of income (this does not include child support, alimony or public assistance). If she expects for you to put out more effort and money just because you have it to satisfy her own unreasonable and selfish expectations, then consider her a liability. **Deduct 1 point.**	
	Total Points Deducted	
PMV	**10** (What is given every female) **minus <Total Points Deducted> =**	

Potential Mate Value (PMV) Chart

Understand that females rate you based upon their spoken (or unspoken) criteria, so it's time for you to start rating them. The PMV chart is a set of general criteria that a man can use as his baseline. You may choose to modify the list to meet your personal preference since you will determine what an acceptable score is.

IMPORTANT NOTE: Just as points are deducted, she can receive REBATES as well. For example, if she has 1 child at home, 1 point is deducted and her PMV drops by 1 point. Once that child is grown and out of the house, she receives 1 REBATE and her PMV increases by 1 point. She can receive rebates in every category except for the "Age" category (unless, that is, she can reverse time). Smile!!

CHAPTER NINE

DeAr Hunting Season
October 31st through February 14th
(Set Your Traps and Take Your Best Shot)

Pre-season -
September 6th through October 30th

Time to 1) survey the grounds where you plan on setting your traps, 2) setting a few pre-season traps just to see how effective you are, 3) modifying your traps, if necessary and 4) being ready when the season begins. Practice your offense as well as your defense (both are important).

IMPORTANT REMINDER: When the season begins, you must check your traps on a regular basis because of poachers. If you don't, they will come around and attempt to steal your DeAr that you may have trapped and left sitting out there defenseless.

Dear Hunting Season

1st quarter -
October 31st through November 30th

The first official day is extremely important and you should be out there if at all possible. Why this day? Because it's Halloween and they tend to really let go and open up. This is the day (at parties especially) that they feel the rush of the season coming on and you have to take advantage of it. You should have your game face on and you should be out there hunting. Don't think about it, go out and do it!!

2nd quarter -
December 1st through December 24th

By now you should be reaping the rewards of your traps because it's getting close to you know what (ho, ho, ho...). Choose DeAr wisely because they are looking for gifts, companionship and emotional support because of the seasonal pressure. They may not really be interested in you in the beginning, but rather just simply caught up in the emotional moment.

Halftime Show -
December 25TH (Christmas Day)

This day should be used to relax, watch some sports, bond with family and get ready for the second half of the season.

3rd quarter -
December 26th through January 15th

This is the time to trap that DeAr that was ignored during the first half of the season. They could possibly be in the frame-of-mind that they will no longer continue to wait on the sidelines as they have been doing and will want to be one of those Valentine's Day recipients. Get rid of the DeAr that you trapped during the first half of the season (that may be either a liability or just too much work) unless they have been fair in providing you what you are expecting to receive.

4th quarter -
January 16th through February 14th

This is the last chance to have a successful hunting season if you haven't already been successful. If you have not caught any DeAr in your traps by the beginning of this quarter, you have to take extreme measures and don't hold back any efforts. You will have to sweeten the bait in your traps or modify your DeAr criteria so that you can end the season with at least one DeAr.

Don't forget to honor our HOLY DAY (Super Bowl Sunday). This is also an excellent day for hunting at those Super Bowl parties.

Dear Hunting Season

Off Season -
February 15th through September 5th

This is the time to first relax, take it easy, bond with other hunters and exchange methods, locations and ideas. Don't waste ANY effort on stray DeAr. If you encounter one, use minimal effort because during the off season they are not as vulnerable. Typically they are usually at an emotional low (or have an attitude) because they did not get the special treatment during the season, may not have had Thanksgiving dinner with someone special, may not have gotten any Christmas gifts, may not have spent New Year's Eve with that special person and lastly may not have gotten a Valentine's Day gift, so they are probably unapproachable at this time. Take the time to evaluate the past season, make the appropriate adjustments and prepare yourselves in any manner you see fit (financially, emotionally, physically, etc.) for the next season.

Remember: A good hunter will not end the season without at least one successful capture.

CHAPTER TEN

Emotionally Stuck on Stupid and No Good for You

Once you have captured that DeAr's attention it is important for you to now closely observe her (them) and see if they qualify as Lemon Law material. Too many good men will either meet or end up with what is typically referred to in the automotive industry as a Lemon. They look good on the outside and have all of the options that you are looking for but their mind is Stuck on Stupid.

Emotionally Stuck On Stupid And No Good For You

Many women today ranging from the under educated, unemployed to the highly educated professionals are Stuck on Stupid and useless to a good man if he is seeking someone to develop a long-term relationship with because they are psychologically and emotionally damaged, drawn to the player, bad boy or abusive types (or dogs as they call them) and prefer the challenge, drama and stress that those types will provide them.

These women will compliment you, the good man, tell you how wonderful you are, how they find you physically attractive, how compatible you are with them but will only be around you until the next (or ex) player or bad boy comes along. These women are not Skeezers but closely related such that the end results with them are the same which would be a waste of your time and energy. When the no good opportunity (because that good opportunity is you) comes along they will bail out on you.

These types of women are stuck on stupid because they won't let go of the players, bad boys or abusive types that they have been with before. To these women those types of men are the ones that make their juices flow and give them those butterflies in their stomach. You can be as good as you want to be or you can be as close to the perfect match for her that she will ever find and she still will not want you.

Here are some of the traits of a female Lemon:

- ✓ She will catch him in his lies and remain with him
- ✓ She dates men that have a wife/woman or multiple women
- ✓ She dates the type that does not let her know where he lives
- ✓ She will spend her time trying to catch him with other women
- ✓ She attaches herself to men that will spend very little time with her
- ✓ She will dump you when he decides that he wants more booty from her
- ✓ She will have sex with him and in many cases be sent home that same night
- ✓ She kills time with you while putting herself on hold waiting for him to come back
- ✓ She breaks up with him and allow him to step right back into her life when he wants to

- ✓ She will spend time to herself or with their girlfriends complaining how he dogged her out

It is very important that if you meet a woman spend a little time with her and begin to develop a personal interested in her that you pop the big question to her at that time. What is the big question you are asking? Well here it is, "Are you emotionally attached to anyone at this time that would hinder our chances of getting to know each other on a personal level?" This will give her the opportunity to either be truthful to you or simply lie to you and most of the time they will lie to you. Either way, the question should be asked because many women are simply player's or bad boy's rejects that are emotionally stuck on stupid and waiting to be recalled by them again. You must recognize those traits so that you will know what you are dealing with. If not, you will become emotionally attached and eventually dumped.

These types of women are everywhere and practices the epitome of stupidity because even when they realize that they made a mistake and passed you over for the player or bad boy, most if not all of them would rather not look back at you and the benefits that the two of you can have but would rather run away and take her chances elsewhere which usually ends up with another player, bad boy or a series of dysfunctional relationships. I believe this is because most women that make these stupid decisions retain that guilt and cannot face you and the truth regarding their selfish and immature decision to bail out on you. Isn't it interesting how most men have no problem in attempting to come back to a good woman when he does the same thing?

    These types of women are mentally ill, need professional therapy and are best left alone for the players, bad boys and drama that they are attracted to.

CHAPTER ELEVEN 11

WHOSO FINDETH A WIFE FINDETH A GOOD THING

That phrase is used quite commonly with women and most (not all) don't know what they are talking about.

First of all, remember that you don't meet a woman and she automatically becomes your wife. If you are not swayed by her looks, then you should know that there is a process that she should follow before she becomes wife potential. I will move from the phrase backwards to help you out if you don't know what I am talking about.

1. Before she can become your wife, she has to **display** wife-like qualities.

2. Before she can **display** wife-like qualities, she has to **know** what those qualities are.

3. Before she can **know** what those qualities are, she has to **learn** those qualities.

4. The way to **learn** those qualities is to be **taught** by a knowledgeable, unselfish and sane individual.

5. Before she can be **taught** those qualities, she has to have the proper **attitude**.

Many women will have grown up with a selfish attitude and will have not been taught what wife-like qualities are. What they do know was probably learned through either "direct, communication from an emotionally damaged and selfish female that made poor choices in her life and now blame men," or have learned through "observation of a dysfunctional relationship," which typically has the man as a financial and material provider of a woman's immature, selfish and emotional demands to simply shut her up and temporarily keep her satisfied; because in most cases that Skeezer will never be satisfied.

Until she can display those wife-like qualities on a consistent basis, all you have found is a thing. You don't know how good that thing is, or if that thing is a good woman that can potentially become your "wife," or just another "Skeezer" that will eventually become a physical, emotional and financial burden.

Unless you are foolish, you should never allow her to bring stress or debt into your life because in time, she shall pass those burdens onto you. Just being a female does not qualify her to be your wife.

If you don't have a clue what those wife-like qualities are, then I suggest you begin with the qualities of a good woman that's in this guide, because if you aren't wise in your choices, you will most likely end up with a "Skeezer".

CHAPTER TWELVE

The Baker's Dozen

For the man that seeks Excitement, Game, Challenge and a Dysfunctional relationship, these 13 personalities below are for you.

These types of women claim to be independent, strong, genuine, reasonable, spiritual/religious, and fair, but in actuality, they are all Skeezers seeking to take advantage of a good man's time, money, and/or resources in one manner or another.

They are pretenders, hypocrites and liars, lazy, irresponsible, inconsiderate, disrespectful, and unreasonable when it comes to their interaction with a good man. Some of them may do well when it comes to doing for themselves, but when it comes to a good man, they will eventually (if not immediately) pass their financial & physical responsibilities onto him.

There is no legitimate reason why any good man should waste his time with these

The Baker's Dozen

types of women once he recognizes them. These types of women have made poor choices in their lives based upon their inconsiderate and selfish thinking. They are now paying the price and looking for a good man to bail them out and should be left for Fools and Players.

You are being officially notified that many of these Skeezers are now in your city or coming soon to you.

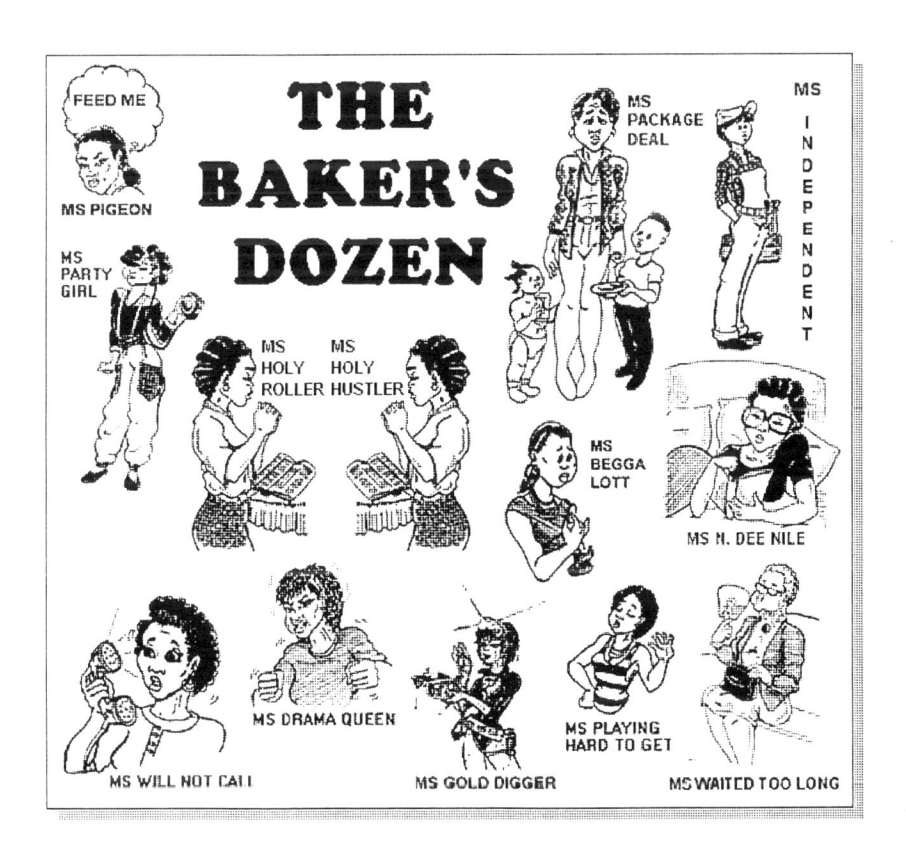

THE BAKER'S DOZEN

- MS PIGEON (FEED ME)
- MS PARTY GIRL
- MS HOLY ROLLER
- MS HOLY HUSTLER
- MS PACKAGE DEAL
- MS INDEPENDENT
- MS BEGGA LOTT
- MS N. DEE NILE
- MS WILL NOT CALL
- MS DRAMA QUEEN
- MS GOLD DIGGER
- MS PLAYING HARD TO GET
- MS WAITED TOO LONG

Be aware that a Skeezer can and probably will have multiple personalities and are experts at deceit.

Their personality can reflect a combination of two or more of the Baker's Dozen, so study them closely and once recognized avoid them at all costs.

Ms Pigeon

Always has an appetite and wants someone to feed her and pay for her meals no matter how much money she has. Has this attitude that you are the man and that you should pay. Tell that CHEAPSKATE you are **THE** man, but not **HER** man. She has no respect for you.

Bridgette is 32 years old, gainfully employed, single with no children. Her philosophy in life is "The more men you meet, the more free meals you will eat."

Bridgette typically will make herself available for men during lunch (11a – 1p) or dinner (7p – 9p). She has not been taught how to be considerate and genuine with a good man and feels whoever invites the other out for a meal to get to know each other should pay. Of course, very seldom (if ever) does Bridgette or women that think like her ever invite a man out. Chances are that she invites (when rarely done) only if she is really interested in him and after he has put out a lot of money on her. Why won't she just say no thanks to men that she is not interested in? It's quite simple she is inconsiderate and does not respect a good man or his money.

Bridgette met Darryl one day while she was making herself available in the mall for some man to approach her and offer to feed her. Darryl was a kind and gentle soul who saw Bridgette, approached her and started up a conversation. They walked through the mall talking and eventually she made her way up to the food court. They ordered and when it came time to pay at the cash register, Bridgette made sure that Darryl was closer to the register than she was. So, as most men are conditioned to do, Darryl paid for both meals. Bridgette never took the time to get to know Darryl beyond him paying for meals.

Bridgette met Ray, another good man, as she was leaving work one day. They talked briefly and Ray asked her if she would like to go and have an early dinner and continue the conversation. Of course she said yes, so they agreed to meet at a familiar restaurant. They met, they ate, they talked and when it came time to pay for the meal, Bridgette looked at Ray and Ray paid for it. Ray suggested that they go on a movie date that weekend and she agreed. Ray picked up Bridgette and they went to the movie theater. Ray paid for the parking, paid for the movie tickets, paid for the concessions and Bridgette never made any efforts to pay for any of the expenses. Bridgette never took the time to get to know Ray beyond him paying for her entertainment expenses.

    Bridgette has no consideration for, respect for or interest in Darryl, Ray or good men like that. Bridgette's interest is in getting men to simply pay for her meals and entertainment, while she puts her money away or spends it on herself.

Ms Drama Queen

The only PEACE you get from her is a GOOD PIECE of ASS. She only feels at her best when she is having sex, acting like a fool in public places or arguing with you.

Monique is 29, single, irresponsible and is attracted to that Bad Boy mentality. She moved away from home when she was 18 and has lived in and out of several places over the years. She is attracted to and submissive to the Bad Boys, and if you don't look or act the part, then she has no interest in you.

When not with a Bad Boy, she spends most of her time watching music videos, going to parties, or talking on the phone to her other girlfriends about the crazy men in their lives.

Monique and her girlfriends were at a party one night where she met Eric and Marcus.

The Baker's Dozen

Eric is 35, responsible and predictable while Marcus is 31, irresponsible and unpredictable.

Eric and a buddy were standing across the room observing Monique. Against his buddy's advice, Eric walked across the room and introduced himself to her. They danced, talked for a while and then Monique asked Eric if he was dating anyone. Eric said that he was not dating anyone presently and gave Monique his phone number and asked her to call him.

Later that evening Monique met Marcus. Marcus had that roughneck look that Monique was attracted to, so she approached Marcus and asked him to dance. They danced for what seemed like an hour without stopping, and afterwards they sat on the couch and talked. Monique asked Marcus if he was dating anyone and Marcus told her that he was dating several women. Monique saw this as a personal challenge and asked him for his number so that she could call him, so he gave it to her. During the next two weeks, Monique spent most of her free time with Marcus at his apartment and a few times he slept overnight at her place. They never went out on a date and then suddenly, Marcus did not have time to spend with her. Monique made numerous attempts to see him, but he simply told her that he was too busy to spend time with her. He explained that he told her when they met that he was dating other women. She continued to harass Marcus until he finally had her served with a restraining order to keep her away.

Four weeks after the party, Eric received a phone call from Monique. They talked and decided to go out on a date. The date, according to Monique, was a disaster. Her complaint was that Eric was not supportive when she talked about how Marcus dumped her, that he was very boring and could not keep her attention. Monique never met with or called Eric again and made excuses for not seeing him when he called.

Monique is now 35 years old and still is a Drama Queen. Good men aren't bad enough and the bad men won't treat her good enough. She is totally misdirected and chances are that she will remain that way.

Ms Begga Lott

Financially irresponsible, broke most of the time and expects you to pay for her financial debts and irresponsible lifestyle. She sometimes will agree to break you off a piece in return but make sure you GET YOURS before or as soon as you pay, because you may not get yours AFTER YOU PAY.

Debra is 26 years old, divorced, good job and no children. Debra has a spending addiction. It's her addiction to spending money that caused her husband to divorce her. She has been in and out of relationships ever since her divorce.

Debra married at 20 and was divorced by the age of 22. Her marriage collapse was because of her spending habits. They were forced to file for bankruptcy, and afterwards her husband filed for divorce.

Debra has never learned her lesson. She spends time dating several men so that they can contribute to paying for her irresponsible financial lifestyle. She has had 3 abortions in 4 years, and sometimes she can't even recall who the potential fathers may have been.

Debra was introduced to Robert through a co-worker. Robert was a pretty stable guy, never married and traveled quite a bit as a sales representative for his company. They had a few dates and he asked her if she was in a relationship with anyone. Debra replied that she was dating but nothing serious. They dated for about 5 months, in between Robert's traveling, and he noticed how difficult it was to contact her when he was away on business. He decided to fly her to the city where he had traveled to for a weekend getaway and while they were having dinner, he expressed to her his interest in starting a monogamous relationship with her since things had been going so well when they would get together. Debra paused, thought about it and then said yes with a smile on her face. They had a great weekend, then she flew back home afterwards.

Concerned about his ability to contact Debra while he was away, Robert hired a private investigator to find out more information about her and to track her daily activities. After 4 weeks, he found out that Debra was deep in debt and still dating several men. Upon receiving that information, Robert never contacted her again.

Today, Debra is still out there living irresponsibly, dating multiple men to get her bills paid.

Ms Independent

She plays the independent GAME well. Has a job (or self-employed), car, an apartment (or house), and claims she doesn't need a man's money. Go out on dates with her and see if she pays for her so-called independent self. Typically she will say "well, he offered to pay," so don't offer and see if she stays. Most of these women require men to make more money than they make to eventually support their lifestyle.

There is a very good chance that these so-called independent women are over-extended financially and would only be a liability to you. The more money that they earn, the more money (credit card debt, etc.) they will spend and will eventually expect you to help them financially.

Nicole is 38 years old, single, never married, self-employed, owns her own home and has everything in life that a woman can want except for a man to call her own. Nicole constantly speaks to her girlfriends about her inability to find a good man that's on her level.

Nicole is a restaurant owner in a trendy part of town. She has unlimited access to good eligible men, but she sees them as beneath her because they don't make the kind of money or live the type of lifestyle that she lives.

Nicole met Jermaine one day at her restaurant. She was talking to one of her employees while he and some buddies were sitting at one of the tables dining. He liked what he saw so he decided to take a chance and see if she would be interested in a date. He approached her, introduced himself and asked her if she would go out on a date with him. She noticed his employee badge on his waist and told him that she was flattered, but was too busy to date anyone at this time. The truth was that she felt that since he was working for someone, he was beneath her level.

Nicole and her girlfriends went out to the club that next evening and again she complained about not meeting any eligible men on her level and that she had more to lose than to gain with men below her. Several men approached her and all of them were rejected for one reason or another.

Just as she was complaining about her lack of choices, Dan entered the club and walked by them. Dan was 42 years old, tall (6' 8"), dark and handsome and the type of man that women dreamed about. Dan was an ex-professional basketball player that is as successful in his business career now as he was in his professional basketball career. He is a certified ladies' man and Nicole knew of Dan, but more importantly, knew of his financial status.

Nicole took it upon herself to go and introduce herself to Dan. Impressed by the sexy dress and the booty, he decided to go with her flow and see what she was up to. They had a few drinks, danced, talked and Dan noticed how Nicole would speak about the men she had met were just not on her level. Dan simply listened to Nicole talk and occasionally nodded his head. Since Dan was giving her the attention, Nicole decided that she was going to be the aggressor and invite him over to her home for a nightcap. Dan accepted; they eventually left the club, and Dan followed her home.

Nicole turned on some soft music, showed Dan where her bar was and told him to get what he wanted while she slipped into something more comfortable. She returned and they shared the wine, soft music and each other for the remainder of the night.

The next morning, Nicole woke up with a hangover, alone in the bed and a note on the other pillow. The note read, "Nicole, I had a great time last night, but I began thinking about those men that you mentioned and some of them are good men that I know personally. Since I have decided to apply your own thinking to you, I now realize that you are beneath my level and that I have more to lose than gain by being with you, so I left. Have a nice day!"

Today Nicole is still very strong, very independent and very much without a man of her own.

Ms Holy Roller

She is waiting on the LORD to send her that mate, but all you have to do is attend church regularly, dress in nice suits so she can be seen with you and accepted by her church peers, spend a little money on her and she will be the BIGGEST FREAK you ever had, BEFORE MARRIAGE, and will justify it by saying that her LORD, THY GOD sent you to her. She possibly has moved from one church to another OR one city to another after sexing those GOD sent men, including YOUR Preachers, Ministers, Bishops and Deacons (Priests are excluded and you already know why).

The Baker's Dozen

Kim is 40 years old, divorced twice and no children. She is a very sweet person but has serious sexual issues when it comes to being in a relationship. Kim was molested as a young teen and was raped by her boyfriend the night of her junior prom. Both occurrences were never reported, and Kim lived in a shell all of those years without receiving any kind of therapy. She became a loner and submerged herself deep into the church and the Lord as a means of getting over her bad experiences.

Kim left her hometown at the age of 19 and worked several jobs in different cities until the age of 25. She was invited to move to Atlanta, by her girlfriend Brandy, so she accepted the invitation. Kim decided to become self-employed as a hair stylist, so she got a part-time job and attended one of the local beauty colleges. She started attending church with Brandy and would attend at least a couple of times a week.

Kim met Brandon while attending the beauty college and they became friends. They spent some time together and talked a lot about what they were going to do after graduation. Kim said that she was going to go and work in the salon where her friend Brandy worked, and Brandon told her that he was going to work in his father's barber shop. There were several occasions when he attempted to get intimate with Kim, but she would tell him that she was not that type of woman and was saved. Brandon was not the church-going type and that bothered Kim since she felt that if he did not go, his soul would not be saved. He eventually stopped spending time with her and only spoke to her at the college.

During the Sunday worship services, Kim would always notice this one particular man that always came to church alone and well dressed. He was tall, handsome and well-groomed. Kim finally got up the nerve to ask Brandy who he was and Brandy told her that his name was Justin. Justin had been noticing Kim, but decided to simply wait her out until the time was right. One day at service, Justin finally decided that since he has seen her at church on a regular basis, it was time to make his move. He approached Kim, introduced himself and told her how it was a blessing to meet her in the church. They sat together during the service and afterwards he invited her and Brandy out to lunch, and Kim was so impressed that he invited both of them that she said yes. They went to lunch and most of the conversation was related to the preacher's sermon. After lunch, Justin asked Kim if he could pick her up next Sunday and accompany him to church. Kim said yes and for the next 3 weeks Kim and Justin would be seen at church together.

Kim decided that since Justin had been such a gentleman all of this time that she would invite him over the next weekend and cook him a meal. Kim told Brandy what she was going to do, and Brandy told her that she would stay at her boyfriend's apartment that weekend so that she and Justin could have the place to themselves. After 6 weeks of dating and Justin being the total gentleman, Kim decided that she did not want to keep him waiting any longer. Kim decided to have a candlelight dinner prepared with wine and soft music when Justin arrived. That evening they wined, dined and Kim eventually surrendered herself to Justin. Kim and Justin dated for about 2 months afterwards, and then Kim started to become very possessive. Justin needed a reason to break away from her and when she started to become possessive, he saw it as his opportunity to get out of the relationship.

Kim was so hurt and embarrassed that she left the church and never returned. She joined another church across town and within a year married one of the deacons. Their marriage lasted about 2 years; after the divorce, Kim packed up her things and moved to another city.

Ms Holy Hustler

She is the hypocritical and psychologically disturbed IDENTICAL twin sister of Ms Holy Roller. She speaks of herself as being prominent in her church and community. She claims that she is a very spiritual person and will present a model image to her Bishop and other members in her church and community to conceal her other personality. The other personality is a cold-hearted hustler and user of any man that she can take advantage of. She is quite skilled in using the "God Game" to gain assets, favors, cash, etc., from men, as well as using that same "God Game" to keep men at a safe, non-sexual but manipulative distance.

Linda is 40 years old, financially overextended and divorced mother of two. She lives in a small town, and her claim is that she was faithful for years to an unfaithful husband. The truth is that her desire was for money and she felt that her husband would some day become rich. When she finally felt that he would not acquire those riches that would give her that lavish lifestyle she desired, she decided that "now" he was unfaithful and it was time to divorce him.

When Linda is not working her day job, she spends time hustling men through the Internet since her town is so small and she feels that no man there can afford her. She has met what she refers to as many prominent men such as doctors, preachers, pilots, businessmen, etc., online, and they have been very good to her. Linda also has a few men in her town that she keeps close enough to her for them to do favors for her. These men in her town are genuine, good men, but simply don't have the wealth she desires. Linda has no sexual desires for a man at all. She is obsessed with a man's money, wealth or potential for money. If you don't have lots of money to spend on her and her children, then she believes that you are wasting her time.

The Baker's Dozen

Linda met Jake online. They had many conversations, and she spoke highly and quite often of her spiritual connection with God. Jake flew to Linda's town to visit her and also paid for a ticket for her to visit him. Between her conversations about God and her failed marriage, Jake developed a warm spot in his heart for her. As time passed, Jake grew closer and closer to Linda and decided to help her with her debts. She spoke of her appreciation until Roman came on the scene, offering her diamonds, cash and a lavish lifestyle. Not only did Roman buy Linda, he also influenced her children by giving them money and things. Linda's claim was that he, Roman, was a gift from God, so she told Jake that either he present her with what Roman has presented her or she had to seriously take time to pray and consider Roman's offer. With that ultimatum from Linda, Jake decided to leave Linda to her destiny with Roman. Ultimately, Roman also pulled away from Linda since he did not get what he wanted.

Well, Linda got her bills paid and got out of debt and she is still hustling men over the Internet, seeking that pot of gold "**In The Name of Jesus.**"

Ms Package Deal

This is Ms So Fine and good looking that in the past (when she had no children), she would not give you, the ordinary guy, the chance at a relationship and now will say to you, "oh, I made a few mistakes." Got knocked up one, two times or more by the Player, Athlete, Doctor, Lawyer or someone she thought was hot and/or that appeared to have money or money potential. Now years later, you look attractive to her. Chances are that if she did not smell the scent of financial relief in you, or if she was younger, she would still never give you an opportunity. Oh yea, remember, the daddy (or daddies) may still be "Spanking That Ass," and especially during the holiday season and birthdays.

Lauren is 35 years old and used to be the life of the party. She knew where all of the parties and prominent social events were and partied from Thursday night until early Sunday morning practically every week. Lauren's intentions had always been to hit the Lottery by getting herself a wealthy man. She would only attend what she referred to as A-Class events. Those were the events where the men were either very financially successful or appeared to be. So far, all she has gotten is knocked up and some child support payments.

    Lauren would attend parties that were given by the A-Class men that she had slept with previously. She met several men at a particular party. One worked at a delivery company, one worked for the city and then there was Matthew. She accepted the phone numbers from all 3 men. She called Matthew the very next day because he told her that night that he was in the music business and would like to go on a date with her. They agreed and the next weekend Matthew picked up Lauren in a limousine and she was extremely impressed. He wined, dined and danced the evening away until closing and afterwards took her back home. Lauren felt as if she had hit the Lottery and was so impressed that she called her girlfriend and they got together for lunch so she could tell her all about it. She said that the other 2 men she met at the party could not compete with Matthew so she was not going to even give them a call. She decided to invite Matthew over to her home the next night for drinks, dinner and a movie. He stayed overnight and left the next morning. Lauren called him several times afterwards, but was not able to contact him. She later found out that she was pregnant, that Matthew lives at home with his mother and that his music business interest is that he sells CDs and DVDs at a music store.

Years, and a couple of children later, Lauren is out there with her package, trying to get one of those ordinary guys that she previously had no interest in to now have an interest in her.

Ms Gold Digger

A CLOSET PROSTITUTE and /or Escort with the idea that you have to pay for the dates if you want to be with her. She typically juggles more than one man at a time and now with the internet, she's a CYBER HO. Bring your credit card, cash and condoms in case you get lucky, don't think you are the only one and leave your heart at home.

Tina is 26 years old, does not have any children and does not want any children because she feels as if they would cramp her lavish lifestyle and considers herself to be an entrepreneur with no desire to enter the "traditional" job market. She is very attractive and knows that there are men out there that will compensate her because of that. She lives a lavish life because of the company of men that she keeps. She not only requires men to compensate her for the sex that she has with them but also she requires them to compensate her for simply the time she spends with them.

Tina spends her free time at places that she knows will have men there with money to spend on her. She has several generous men that she spends time with, and all of them compensate her well for her time. Her men are typically at least 20 to 25 years older, and she thinks that at their ages, they are just willing to cut through the chase and pay for what they want.

Tina was introduced to the Internet and singles' Websites by her girlfriend and had no previous knowledge about them. She spent several hours with her girlfriend showing her how she could join those sites and have access to even more men. Tina convinced one of her men to buy her a computer and set her up with Internet service at her condo. Her explanation to him was that she could send him email from time to time and stay in contact with him when he is away on business.

Once Tina learned her way through the different sites, she decided to upgrade her quality of men and use them to travel to different states and countries. She posted some suggestive photos on the different Websites and the responses were overwhelming. So overwhelming that Tina soon found that she did not have time for the men she presently had, so she dumped all but the man that was paying for her Internet service since he traveled a lot and did not interfere with her travels to see these other men.

Tina has accumulated a sizeable bank account, travels to other states at least 2 weekends out of the month and travels out of the country at least 3 times a year.

Tina's philosophy is that life is too short to be around men that cannot afford her desired lifestyle.

Ms Playing Hard To Get

(TEASE) – For the man that wants nothing in life but to waste time, this one lives for the attention only. She knows from first contact that she has no interest in you and enjoys keeping you in suspense. She will let you get just close enough to keep you around to get her ego stroked.

Thedra is 33 years old, a single mother of a 2 year old and has a psychopathic personality. Thedra is just another hood rat with a job that believes that she has a relationship with her baby's daddy so she really doesn't allow men to get close to her. She believes, in her mind, that she and her baby's daddy will someday live together, but in reality, she was simply an easy booty call. Thedra loves attention so she will allow men to get just close enough to think that they have a chance.

Thedra has a couple of girlfriends but none of them are so close to her that she allows them into her private life. They have never seen her with the baby's daddy, and sometimes they wonder if she even knows who the daddy is.

Maria is Thedra's closest friend, that is, when the two of them are getting along with each other. The two of them grew up together and according to Maria, Thedra has always been a little strange. Thedra has a Caucasian fixation, but none of them accepts her for more than a booty call.

Thedra gets that psychopathic personality off by having good men display an interest in her, spend time with her and then she dumps them or they get tired of her games and leave. She has had several good men interested in her, but they were never good enough for more than someone to give her attention or take her out. Anytime one of those good men would express an interest in getting closer to her, she would come up with some excuse to avoid getting into that type of relationship with them. She is in love with the man of her dreams, and little does she know that the man of her dreams is just another player that plays the game well.

A GOOD MAN'S SURVIVAL GUIDE

Thedra types are best suited for players, so leave them to their fantasy of waiting for their baby's daddy to return.

Ms Party Girl

She lives in the world of fantasy, fun & recreation. Typically, she is the young cutie that's looking for that man that will allow her to continue to live that irresponsible, childish lifestyle. What she refuses to see is that with time and receiving all the attention, she will go from that YOUNG, FIRM CUTIE to that OLE', LOOSE BOOTY CALL that no one will commit to.

Angela is 28, single, lives at home and has no children. She has always been a daddy's girl. Her mother and father never taught her responsibility, and they have always given her what she wants. She has had the cars, clothes and freedom to do whatever she wants to do. Angela's philosophy is that she does not like to live by rules. She does what she wants, when she wants and how she wants, and if any man does not like it, then he should not be around her. Angela spends most of her free time partying, going on dates that the men must pay for or just hanging around the house.

Angela has a job only so that she can have money to support her entertainment when men aren't paying for it. She does not remain in any type of relationship with a man because she says that they can't keep her attention long enough and she gets bored fast. Her parents have bailed her out financially numerous times due to her irresponsible attitude with money.

One day Angela met Keith, the man of her dreams. They had lunch, talked and laughed about the things that they had in common, and it seemed as if Angela finally was ready to show some stability in her life. She decided to remove all of the other men out of her life and become available to Keith whenever he wanted to see her. Keith and Angela decided to get an apartment together. They lived together for about 6 months and after Keith noticed that Angela was not participating in keeping the apartment clean, not helping out with paying the bills and constantly wanting to go to parties, he felt that it was time to leave. He moved out and Angela moved back home to her parents. Angela has moved in and out of her parent's home at least 4 times in the last 2 years.

Today, Angela is still living that life of a party girl, her parents are still paying her bills and she is still looking for the man that will give her that free ride.

Ms Will Not Call

Collecting phone numbers to her is all a GAME and she has no plans on calling you. In reality, that is quite inconsiderate since you are expecting to receive a phone call from her. If you call her and she asks you to call her back because she is on the phone or you don't hear from her within 1 week of giving her your number, don't take her calls serious because remember, to her it's simply just a game. If after a couple of calls she doesn't give you her number, DUMP HER.

Carla is 32 years old, single, very immature and no children. The 3 most important things in Carla's life are "attention, attention and more

The Baker's Dozen

attention." She gets her ego stroked by controlling the flow of communication with men. In most cases, she will not initially give you her phone number and may accept yours knowing that you are expecting her to call you. That expectation of you hearing from her gives her an egotistical rush.

Carla plays with anywhere from 4 to 8 men in any given month. She will, from time to time, give her number out to a few men, but when they call, she may say something like, "I'm on the phone call me back." Now that makes absolutely no sense at all since you don't know when she will finish her phone call. What she is indirectly telling you is that "she does not value you." You should accept her lack of interest and move on.

There are a couple of men that Carla calls, but neither of those men have any interest in her other than for a booty call. If either of those two men call her while she is on the phone, she will immediately release you and talk to them. Carla is good at recognizing men that will put up with her foolishness, such as men like George and James.

George has called Carla at least 4 times in 2 days and has left a couple of messages asking her to call him back. She has intentionally not returned his calls because she does not value him.

James has called her and because she can see his number on her caller id, she does not pick up. Her excuse to him is that she was not feeling good for a few days and did not feel like talking. The truth is that she was a booty call for a couple of days and did not want to be disturbed.

Carla has these insecure men wrapped around her little finger. Don't let it happen to you because there are good women out there that will respect you and value the interest that you have in them.

Ms N. Dee Nile

(WAITING FOR EX) – Here is the CLASSIC case of being in DENIAL. She is waiting for one of her EX's (could be her babies' daddy) because the Look, Sex and/or Money was too good to let go of and she wants only him. Do not waste your time because her EX may be periodically making a booty call or spending a little time with her to make sure she does not go to someone else. Trust me, she will not tell him no and will kick you to the curb or put you on hold as soon as she gets that call from him.

Stephanie is a 38-year-old single mother with a 4-year-old child and has never been married.

She met Michael about 10 years ago and their relationship had been off and on for the last 6 of those 10 years.

Stephanie has met several good men during her off and on relationship with Michael, but she never seems to stay away, physically or emotionally, from Michael long enough to get to know any other man and develop a meaningful relationship with any of them. Instead, all Michael has to do is, literally, blow his whistle, and she comes running back to him.

Prior to Stephanie getting pregnant, she met Mark one day at the movies. Mark was about 15 years older than Stephanie. He saw Stephanie standing in the concession line at the movie theatre so he approached her and said hello with a warm smile. She reciprocated with a warm smile as well and a hello as she waited for her turn to make her purchase. In their brief conversation, Mark asked her what movie she was going to see and it turned out that they were there to see the same movie. Mark wasted no time inquiring as to whether or not she was in a relationship with anyone. Stephanie told him yes and so he left and went into the movie theatre alone to watch the movie. After the movie was over, he decided to again ask

Stephanie if she was in a relationship. She said no and explained that she said that because she was tired of men approaching her and asking her that question. Mark talked with her as he walked her to her car and they exchanged phone numbers. By the time they reached her car, they decided to go and get a bite to eat. They spent the next few months getting to know each other and then one day Stephanie told Mark that she was, again, going back to live with her ex, Michael.

A year passed and Mark was told, through a mutual friend, that he had seen Stephanie and that she was pregnant. Well, Stephanie became a mother and her relationship with Michael lasted about 6 to 8 months after she had the baby. She felt that even though their relationship was dysfunctional, she thought that having a child would make things better between the two of them. Stephanie and the child eventually moved out into her own place.

Today, Stephanie is still emotionally connected to Michael, killing time with good men that she has no genuine interest in and waiting for her baby's daddy to return to her and their child.

Ms Waited Too Long

She waited years to exhale with him and eventually the man she waited for ended up committing to another woman. Typically, after waiting too long, she becomes bitter, develops an attitude and dates younger men claiming that she does not want a relationship and just wants to have some fun, but in reality, she is lying to herself and others. The younger man will have a good time "Spanking That Ass" until he decides he wants a committed relationship or marriage and in most cases, will leave her for a woman his age or younger than he is.

Yvonne was 25 years old, energetic, attractive and had just been promoted to assistant manager on her job when she met Aaron, who was 30 and recently divorced. They talked briefly and exchanged phone numbers. Yvonne called Aaron a few days later and invited him to lunch on Saturday. They spent the entire day and evening together, talking and enjoying each other's company before Aaron returned Yvonne to her apartment. As time progressed, they developed a very close friendship and Yvonne was emotionally growing closer and closer to Aaron. They would go out to dinner, go dancing, go to concerts and take little weekend trips together. Yvonne and Aaron dated for about 3 years before she brought up the big question, "Are we going to get married?" Aaron replied that he was not ready to jump back into a marriage, and that he was happy with her the way things were.

Yvonne met several good men that expressed a personal interest in getting to know her, but she remained faithful to the idea of her and Aaron one day getting married. Yvonne decided that she would not give up on Aaron and convinced him that they should get an apartment together; hoping that being physically together would change his mind about marriage. They lived together for 10 years and during that time Yvonne would, on occasion, complain to Aaron about his refusal to marry her. Again, he would tell her that he was not interested in marriage.

Eventually Yvonne, now 38, decided that this was not the type of relationship that she wanted so she left Aaron. Then she met Walter, who was 48, and they had a few dates. Yvonne's complaint was that Walter was too structured, predictable and boring and that she was looking for more excitement in her life, so she never dated Walter again.

About eight months had passed before Yvonne received a call from a girlfriend that told her she heard that Aaron was engaged and getting married. Yvonne was devastated and began dating younger men for the next 12 years and would always say that she was not interested in love and relationships and just wanted to have fun. Regardless of her spoken words, she secretly desired a relationship with many of the younger men she dated, but nothing ever materialized beyond dates and casual sex. Yvonne eventually became frustrated and gave up on men and dating.

Yvonne is now 65 years old, never married and spends much of her time either alone at home with her pets or going to church to keep busy.

Yvonne finally got to the point where she regrets waiting so long for Aaron and ignoring the many good men that had an interest in her. Unfortunately, it was now too late for her because no man, good or no good, has an interest in her.

CHAPTER THIRTEEN

How to TRANSLATE for a Good Man

Woman says:
I would like for us to try and be friends first.

Translation:
I am not that attracted to you, so I would like to see how much use you would be to me before I decide if I want to keep you around me.

Woman says:
I like you but I don't want to ruin our friendship.

Translation:
I have no personal interest in you. I like what you do for me (no sex, of course) so I want to keep you at a distance just in case I do meet someone that I am interested in.

Woman says:
I can't find a good man.

How To Translate For A Good Man

Translation:
I can't find a man that will obey me and do what I say.

Woman says:
I don't have any single girlfriends.

Translation:
I have single girlfriends but not any that I would introduce to you.

Woman says:
I don't like a cheap man.

Translation:
If you want to spend time with me, you will have to spend your money on me.

Woman says:
I would like someone who is very intelligent, sweet, romantic, respected, generous and spiritual.

Translation:
Very Intelligent – You should earn a large enough income to be spent on me; **Sweet** – You should want me so badly that you will do whatever I request; **Romantic** – You should

provide me with that fantasy, storybook lifestyle I dream of that I am too lazy or irresponsible to provide for myself; **Respected** – You should be admired by others so that it makes me look good being with you; **Generous** – You shall give me gifts, help pay my bills and expenses and support my irresponsible lifestyle; **Spiritual** – I have no idea what the hell this means but it sounds good saying it.

Woman says:
I will not have sex until after I am married.

Translation:
I have dated men, I have had sex with all the men I was attracted to and they still did not marry me, so now I am going to use God or my frustration in making bad choices as my sexual shield. Since you don't have the fame, fortune or looks, I am not that physically attracted to you so I will make you wait.

Woman says:
I make and have my own money.

Translation:
I make and have my own money, but I am not going to spend it if I am with you. That is what your money is for.

Woman says:
I am not interested in shallow men and I do not have friends who are.

Translation:
I can't handle rejection and especially if you are not physically attracted to me. I will never introduce you to any of my girlfriends that you may be attracted to. If I can't be happy with you I will make sure that none of them will be.

CHAPTER FOURTEEN

IF YOU HAVE TO PAY, IT'S ALL ABOUT HER

Relationships, simply stated, are "how we interact" with each other. We can do so on a Personal, Social or Business relationship level.

An "admission fee" (requires money, services or goods) for time or services rendered establishes a business relationship and, in most cases, will corrupt the probability of developing a loving and meaningful personal relationship. This is the mentality of the women that have been raised to think and/or behave like CLOSET prostitutes. In other words, "don't take it personal, it's just business."

An OVERT (street or call girl) prostitute gets her orgasm through "compensation" (money & goods) and not "appreciation" (just happy to be in your company). The sexual high is a bonus. There are very little (if any) feelings associated with you. It's your compensation that she is feeling, so there is no need to attempt to cater to the prostitute's feelings other than by compensating her. You don't have to repair things for her; take her to dinner, plays, movies or any other social events. If you have paid an "admission fee" then it is strictly a "business transaction" (relationship) to her.

The same should apply to the Covert (closet) prostitute. If you have to pay then it will be all about her. She may pretend to care if she thinks that will help get her what she wants, but in actuality it means nothing to her. That covert mentality is not much different than the overt mentality, with the exception that the overt will give you what you expect on a consistent basis as long as you are paying as opposed to the covert, that will give you what she wants to give you, even after you have paid. If you don't think the covert prostitute's mentality is the same as the overt prostitute's then stop paying an admission fee and see what happens to you.

I have observed 3 basic types of women that charge an admission fee. A prostitute does not have to sell just sexual services. A prostitute can sell just her time being with you, which means that you will have to pay for the expenses if you want to spend time with her.

1. OVERT - This is their livelihood. They eat, sleep and breathe this behavior. In most cases, they will give you exactly what you want as long as you are paying the admission fee.

2. CLOSET - This is their second livelihood (or third depending on the number of jobs they have to compensate for their financial irresponsibility or lavish lifestyle). They can be a skilled worker, a degreed professional, an unskilled worker or unemployed. Chances are that you may get what you pay for, in the beginning, but eventually, it will subside to a reduced effort on their part, while the compensation expectations will continue to grow.

3. BITCH - This one you definitely want to recognize ASAP! This one expects you to pay that admission fee and has no intentions on giving you anything. This one will receive and label you as a friend as quickly as possible and from that point on, you are SUCKERMAN.

If You Have To Pay, It's All About Her

The only relationship that these women want when they require an admission fee from you is a business relationship, so you should never desire a personal relationship or develop feelings for a woman that thinks like any of the 3 above.

DO NOT FEEL SPECIAL because you were given the opportunity, by her, to spend your money on her. If you have to spend your money on her, then she does not value you as a person anyway. She values what she can get out of you and will juggle between you and her other foolish good men that she has.

CHAPTER FIFTEEN

DOES SHE GENUINELY WANT TO BE YOUR FRIEND?

Ever hear these words.... "Let's Just Be FRIENDS?" That's the ultimate in Sexual Rejection. It means that a woman (I am speaking of single, unattached and available) typically has absolutely no sexual interest in you. Now being just friends will be fine, if you also have no personal or sexual interest in her. I will caution you to not put yourself in denial, thinking that she will change her mind about you. If you do that and she is a Skeezer, you are going to be a tool to be used at her convenience, not yours.

Here is how you can prove whether or not her interest in becoming your friend is genuine. Since she claims she wants to be just friends with you and you have agreed, tell her that you....

Does She Genuinely Want To Be Your Friend?

1. Want to meet all of her single female friends and she will tell the ones you are attracted to, in yours and their presence, that she has no personal interest in you and that you are just friends. If she claims she has no single female friends then you must ask her what are the benefits for you in becoming friends with her (this is very important).

2. Will not be wasting your time listening to her complain or talk about other men she is interested in.

3. Will treat her the same as your male and other platonic female friends.

4. Only do special favors for those that do the same for you and it will not be one-sided.

5. Don't do things for her that you would do for a woman that you are intimately involved with.

6. Don't do things for her that she would expect from a man she is intimately involved with. Tell her to go and get her own man for those things, because after all, she is your friend and should

be able to take honest and direct communication from you.

7. Will not spend money on her so don't expect it to happen.

The things above will eliminate 95 percent (nothing's perfect) of the Skeezers out of your life (unless you are seeking to be used). If she agrees to (and abides by) those things above, then she truly wants to be your friend. If she doesn't, she's a Skeezer so dump her and move on. Your life and time is far more important and it would be better for you to be away from her than to waste your time with her. Always remember that there are good women out there who can establish a genuine friendship, if that's what you are seeking.

CHAPTER SIXTEEN 16

DAH PLAYAZ KLUB — WE GET OURS AND THEN SOME

Charm Her
Couch Potato
No Mo' Money
Mama's Boy
Handy Man
Pulpit Pimp
Player
Gigga Her Lo
Procrastinator
Sugar Daddy
Down Low
Won't Let Go

These are the men that get most of the good women. The men in the Klub are the ones that good women are initially attracted to and then later on they complain the most about to good men. Take time to study each Playaz description.

The reason why most good women aren't available is because they allow the men of Dah Playaz Klub into their lives most of the time. I have found that many of these good women are attracted to Excitement, Game & Challenge so they tend to see the good man who is Predictable, Reliable & Stable as Boring. Notice how close the Pulpit Pimp and Player are standing next to each other. That is no accident.

Charm Her

He is a challenge to his own ego and doesn't necessarily want the sex. He knows that most women will fall for the Prince Charming fantasy (flowers, cards, dinners and lot's of attention). After he's gotten that "Egotistical Orgasm," he will move on to the next woman leaving her in that emotional void.

Couch Potato

He gives the television, food and couches more attention that he does her but she is convinced that she can change his ways. Chances are she found him like that, considered him to be one that was not as physically attractive as other men, and knew she would have him all to herself without other women trying to steal him from her. Now, after a child or 2 or 3, she is stuck and disappointed.

No Mo' Money
(The Fool)

Yep, he figured that he was ALL THAT because he was spending money on women, and they were spending time with him. Well, once he lost his job and the money ran out, so did the women. The key is, don't let the money run out FOOL and you will continue to have the women around you that want you for your money.

Sugar Daddy

He's got it all together and has a few women that he regularly visits. He does not want a commitment and is only looking for a good time and will pay for it. Typically he looks for the woman under 35 years old and considers a woman over 35 too old for him.

Pulpit Pimp
(The President of the Klub; the Top Dog)

He has the tightest GAME in town. Women are standing in line waiting on their chance to let him LAY HANDS (and whatever else he wants) ON or INSIDE of them to BLESS them. He has a wife that probably knows about his game but is not giving up the material perks, ego stroke and ENVY from other women, so she accepts his behavior. He may have money or the illusion of money, a home, prominence and a regular Sacrificial Offering of "Cleavage, Tits and Ass" on the side. He's the only PLAYA that can get that "Quick Cash" and "Spank That Ass," without any effort, be forgiven and the other women will literally stand in line waiting for their turn. He is the "Smoothest Operator in the Klub" and even the Player's game is not as tight as the Pulpit Pimp's game.

Player

This one is quite skilled at the GAME and loves it, although he can't compete with the Pulpit Pimp. Some Players have converted to the pulpit to get that "Quick Cash" and "Spank That Ass" whenever they want to. The Player sees it all as a sport and is usually the quicker thinker in the Klub. He knows all of the lines and is extremely skilled at reading a woman's body language. The Player "Knows When to Quit" and will only take his game so far. If he does not get the results that he is looking for, he is on to the next one.

Mama's Boy

If you truly love a CHALLENGE, this is the one for you. The mama's boy does not want to leave home and simply prefers the security that his parent(s) provide. He does not take life's responsibilities seriously. He will work just enough to get by and may even try to live off of you, if he gets the chance to move in with you.

Gigga Her Lo
(Gigolo)

Here is, the "Younger Man" that older women love to brag about to men her age or older. He will do what she wants, how she wants it, and when she want it, as long as she will provide money and goods for him. Chances are that she will boast to her girlfriends about him AND as long as she is putting out, he will be around (and I don't mean for the sex, because he has someone else that satisfies him). His objective is MONEY and/or GOODS and if he gets the Sex, it's just a bonus but not expected. If asked about him, she usually replies, "Oh, he's My Friend."

Handy Man

Now here is where you can get ALMOST all of what you want except COMMITMENT. He is quite skilled with his hands (and other parts of his body as well) and has many homes that he takes care of. He prides himself in his work (the work that he does around the house, on your car and the work that he does on you). He is better than a plumber because when he leaves your home, YOUR PIPES and the pipes in your home are cleared and you are left waiting for the next visit.

Procrastinator

He is a professional planner. Tells you about his life and what he is going to do, or what he wants to do but never really finishes it. He is afraid to take any risks and would rather play it safe. If he is lucky, you will be overwhelmed with his looks and the way he performs sexually, so that when it's time to question his progress, he will simply give you another good STIFF one and that will again satisfy you for the moment.

Won't Let Go

Immature, possessive, selfish and in denial —all rolled up into one. Extremely attentive, in the beginning, which he knows women love. He is good at lying, listening to women talk, and feeding back to them just what they want to hear. He tends to be very controlling and will run most (if not all) of her friends or family members away if given the opportunity.

Down Low
(DL)

He is either married, involved or has multiple women. Will spend time with you, can hold a conversation just as long as any woman can, will spend money on you, but will not be seen in certain public places with you, depending on his situation. By the way, for you women IN DENIAL, yes he is involved SEXUALLY with other men.

CHAPTER SEVENTEEN

BUSY OR UNAVAILABLE IS JUST AN EXCUSE

You should unselfishly value yourself. Your life is measured in and expires with time. Time is irreplaceable & life is precious because "Time is Life and as Time goes so does your Life". If that's the case and you value your life then don't foolishly waste time waiting on (or wanting) a woman that does not value you. Since time waits for no one, why would you foolishly do so?

Now, where am I going with that? Well, first let me do what most should before I make my point, which is, define some key words that I will use so that there is a clear understanding:

Busy Or Unavailable Is Just An Excuse

Busy — is full of activity and **Unavailable** — is not capable of being used or seen.

    We all have activity in our lives. I typically like to use the phrase; "Activity with no productivity" which means many of us are doing a whole lot of nothing (which, of course, a person has the right to do).

    Busy (activity) is a necessity in order to accomplish things in our lives, so if you aren't busy, then you aren't accomplishing a thing.

    Unavailable is a choice that you make for whatever reason.

    No one is so busy that they are unavailable. They just choose to be unavailable for you because they don't value you. Yea, I know that the truth hurts, but it can set you free.

    Remember that the next time you have an interest in a woman and she tells you that she is "really busy" or "don't have the time." Read between the lines and accept that what she is really saying is she don't value you. Just remember:

- ✓ Don't get angry at her.
- ✓ Don't de-value yourself as she has done you.

- ✓ Don't sit around waiting for her to have time.

- ✓ Don't try to convince her to spend time with you.

- ✓ Don't question why she don't have time, because I have already told you why.

- ✓ Don't make yourself available for her since she isn't doing it for you.

- ✓ Don't allow her or yourself to make excuses for not spending time with you.

- ✓ Do move on and away from her mentally and physically IMMEDIATELY.

- ✓ Do value yourself and know that other women out there will value you.

- ✓ Do get out of denial thinking that she is interested in you and does value you.

- ✓ Do not think that you can just be friends if you have a personal interest in her.

- ✓ Do question her "now I'm available" motives. There is a chance she may still not value you and is just killing time with you since the person she wants does not value her. You will be dumped eventually.

Unselfishly (not at the expense of others) value yourself; because each minute you lose waiting on a so-called "busy" woman, is a minute out of your life. I know most of you good men will wait mentally by just killing time with others until that person pretends to now value you. Realize that there are good women out there that you can be attracted to so don't wait on Ms. Busy, because if she valued you she would spend time getting to know you.

CHAPTER EIGHTEEN

THE KEY TO PEACE OF MIND, PRODUCTIVITY AND LONGEVITY IS CLEANSING

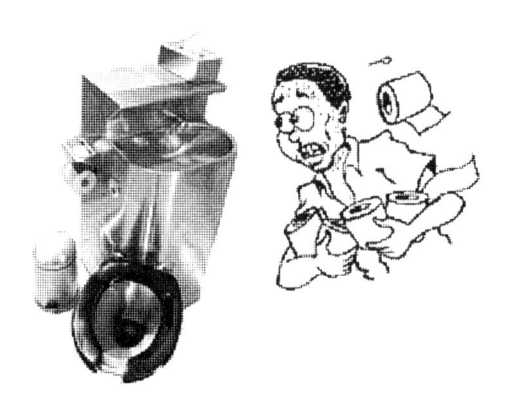

Take some quality time to evaluate your life and dispose of the toxic waste in your life. I am speaking about the people and things that drain your time, energy and finances.

If you don't go through this cleansing process, then shut up, stop complaining about

The Key to Peace of Mind, Productivity and Longevity is Cleansing

those toxic women or things, accept the drain and drama that they bring and don't burden others with your waste that you choose to not let go of.

Remember that you do have a CHOICE.

BOOK AVAILABLE THROUGH
Milligan Books, Inc.

A Good Man's Survival Guide
Price: $13.95

Order Form

Milligan Books, Inc.
1425 W. Manchester Ave., Suite C, Los Angeles, CA 90047
(323) 750-3592

Name_____ Date_____
Address _____
City _____ State_____ Zip Code _____
Day Telephone _____
Evening Telephone _____
E-Mail _____
Book Title _____
Number of books ordered _____ Total $_____
Sales Taxes (CA Add 8.25%) $_____
Shipping & Handling $4.90 for one book $_____
Add $1.00 for each additional book $_____
Total Amount Due $_____
☐ Check   ☐ Money Order   ☐ Visa   ☐ MasterCard
☐ Other Cards _____Expiration Date _____
Credit Card No._____
Driver License No._____
       Make check payable to Milligan Books, Inc.

Signature _____ Date_____